re to be

VOYAGES OF DISCOVERY

Exploring the
POLAR
Regions

Editor April McCroskie

Author Jen Green

Illustrated by David Antram

Produced by The Salariya Book Company Ltd
25, Marlborough Place, Brighton, England

© The Salariya Book Company Ltd

First published in 1997 by
Macdonald Young Books, an imprint of
Wayland Publishers Ltd
61 Western Road
Hove
East Sussex
BN3 1JD

Find Wayland on the internet
at http://www.wayland.co.uk

A catalogue record for this book is available
from the British Library.

ISBN 0-7500-2122-5

Printed in Hong Kong

Exploring the
POLAR
Regions

Jen Green

David Antram

MACDONALD YOUNG BOOKS

CONTENTS

INTRODUCTION

The polar regions are the coldest, most hostile places on Earth. For centuries legends and rumours circulated about these unknown lands. Early maps of the Arctic showed the North Pole as a high black rock rising from an icy ocean surrounded by four great islands. Nothing at all was known for certain about Antarctica. Legends spoke of a vast, uncharted land called *Terra Australis Incognita*, which means "unknown south land", split in two by a frozen sea. The region was thought to be inhabited by devils, ghosts and monsters, and all ships that sailed there were doomed.

Yet from the 10th century a few bold people began to visit the Arctic and later Antarctica. They went there in search of land, to seek out new sea routes for trade and to discover the unknown. Later they struggled to reach the Poles, for their own glory and for the glory of their countries. Their stories are tales of great courage and endurance in the face of terrible hardship. Many died of cold or hunger on these expeditions. Some returned to the warmth and safety of their homes, but remembered the desolate beauty of the polar regions and longed to return. This book tells the stories of the heroic adventurers who faced the harshest conditions on Earth to explore these awesome, icy lands.

The Polar Regions

The polar regions are the areas around the North and South Poles, imaginary points which mark the most northerly and the most southerly limits of the Earth. The Arctic is named after a northern constellation of stars, the bear, which in Greek is *arktos*. Antarctic means "the opposite of Arctic". The magnetic poles lie near the geographic poles.

The Sun's rays are weakest in the polar regions, making them among the coldest places on Earth. For most of the year, the seas are ice-covered and the land lies under ice and snow. As the Earth moves around the Sun each year, one Pole is tilted towards the Sun and the other is tilted away from it.

So both the Arctic and Antarctic experience a time in summer during which the sun never sets, and a period in winter when it never rises. Because of the continual daylight in midsummer, these regions are called the lands of the midnight sun.

But there are many differences between the polar regions too. The Arctic is an ice-covered ocean surrounded by land, where a jigsaw of ice-sheets, called floes, drifts slowly in the deep sea currents. The Antarctic (or Antarctica) is a vast land mass, the fifth-largest continent on Earth, surrounded by seas that are also mostly ice-covered. Plants grow in some parts of the Arctic, and there is more varied wildlife; Antarctica is a huge icy desert with little vegetation. Since prehistoric times people such as the Inuit (Eskimos) and Saami (Lapps) have lived in the Arctic. Antarctica has never been inhabited.

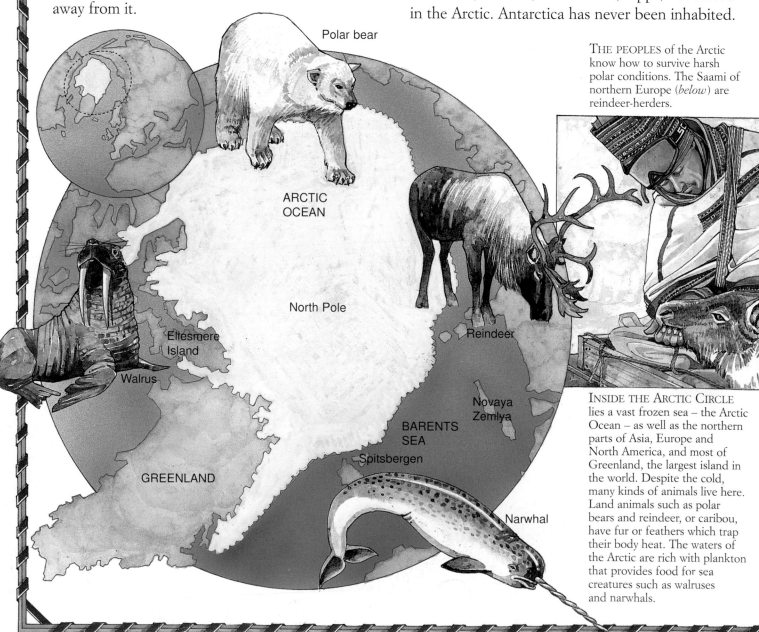

THE PEOPLES of the Arctic know how to survive harsh polar conditions. The Saami of northern Europe (*below*) are reindeer-herders.

Polar bear

ARCTIC OCEAN

North Pole

Walrus

Ellesmere Island

Reindeer

Novaya Zemlya

BARENTS SEA

Spitsbergen

GREENLAND

Narwhal

INSIDE THE ARCTIC CIRCLE lies a vast frozen sea – the Arctic Ocean – as well as the northern parts of Asia, Europe and North America, and most of Greenland, the largest island in the world. Despite the cold, many kinds of animals live here. Land animals such as polar bears and reindeer, or caribou, have fur or feathers which trap their body heat. The waters of the Arctic are rich with plankton that provides food for sea creatures such as walruses and narwhals.

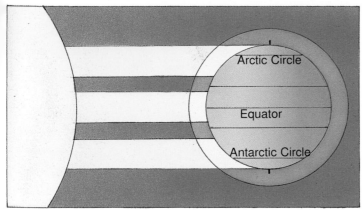

THE SUN'S RAYS strike the Earth most intensely at the Equator, and least intensely at the Poles. Here, the curve of the Earth means the rays are spread out over a wider area. At the Poles sunlight also has farther to travel through Earth's atmosphere, which absorbs much of the heat before it reaches the surface. The Arctic and Antarctic Circles are imaginary circles that run parallel to the Equator and mark the borders of the polar regions.

TWO HUNDRED YEARS AGO Antarctica was unknown. The continent is still being explored and mapped today. It is covered by a permanent ice cap over four kilometres thick in places. It has never been inhabited, and scientists who live there today are dependent on the outside world for supplies. But because Antarctica is unknown and unpolluted, it is of great scientific interest. Research bases have been established by many countries. Their research ships (*below*) patrol the seas.

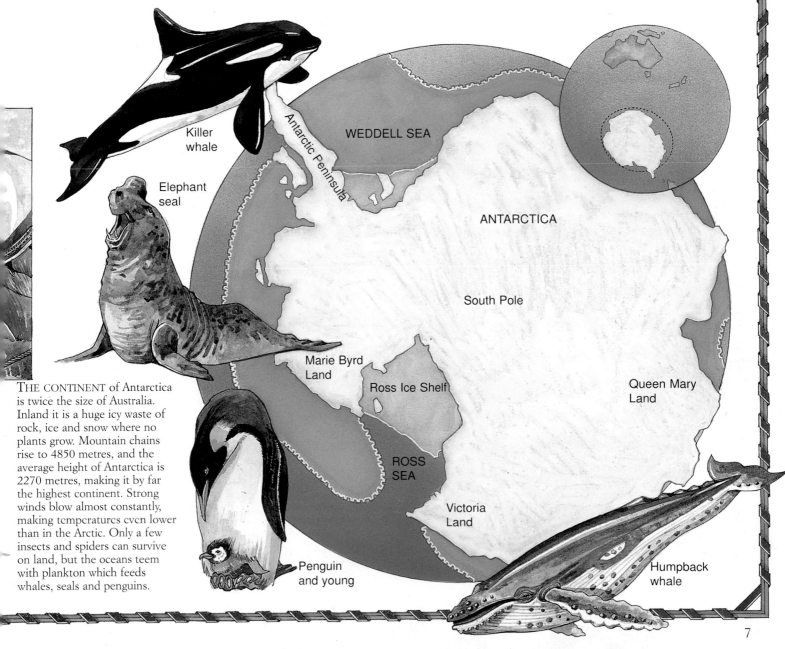

THE CONTINENT of Antarctica is twice the size of Australia. Inland it is a huge icy waste of rock, ice and snow where no plants grow. Mountain chains rise to 4850 metres, and the average height of Antarctica is 2270 metres, making it by far the highest continent. Strong winds blow almost constantly, making temperatures even lower than in the Arctic. Only a few insects and spiders can survive on land, but the oceans teem with plankton which feeds whales, seals and penguins.

Killer whale

Elephant seal

Penguin and young

WEDDELL SEA

Antarctic Peninsula

ANTARCTICA

South Pole

Marie Byrd Land

Ross Ice Shelf

Queen Mary Land

ROSS SEA

Victoria Land

Humpback whale

7

Vikings in the Arctic

The first European peoples to visit the Arctic were Irish monks of the 8th century, who braved the North Atlantic in tiny boats, in search of solitude. They reached Iceland around AD 770. Around the same time, the Viking peoples of Scandinavia in northern Europe began to explore the northern seas in search of new lands to farm. They reached Iceland in AD 874, and by AD 930 as many as 10,000 Vikings had settled there.

Around AD 900, a Viking called Gunnbjorn was caught in a great storm off Iceland. His ship was blown westwards, to a land with high cliffs. After the storm Gunnbjorn returned to Iceland. In AD 982 a Viking called Erik the Red was exiled from Iceland for three years. He decided to explore the land Gunnbjorn had described. He sailed west and eventually sighted a rocky coast with towering fiords and green pastures. Erik named his discovery "Greenland". In AD 986 he returned to the new land with 15 ships. Soon more settlers arrived. They built houses and traded with the Inuit peoples of Greenland. In summer they farmed, and in winter they hunted and fished. But gradually the climate of Greenland began to change. Temperatures grew colder and ice began to cover more of the land. There were clashes between the remaining settlers and the Inuit peoples, and by 1400, the Viking colonies on Greenland had died out.

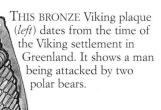

THIS BRONZE Viking plaque (*left*) dates from the time of the Viking settlement in Greenland. It shows a man being attacked by two polar bears.

DURING the 9th and 10th centuries Viking explorers reached Iceland and Greenland. They also crossed the Norwegian Sea as far as the Kola Peninsula. From the 8th century raiding parties visited Britain.

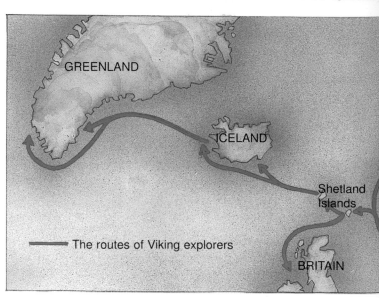

GREENLAND

ICELAND

Shetland Islands

— The routes of Viking explorers

BRITAIN

The Vikings search for new lands.

GOOD FARMING LAND was scarce in Scandinavia. The Vikings sailed the stormy waters of the North Atlantic west of Scandinavia in search of new lands where they could farm and graze their herds. They established two settlements in Greenland, one on the east coast and the other around the island's southern tip at Eriksfjord. Migrating Viking colonists travelled in ships called *knarrs*. These boats were broader and shallower than the warring longships that were used on raiding parties, so there was plenty of room for passengers and cargo.

Kola Peninsula

SCANDINAVIA

THE VIKINGS were skilful sailors. They used a device called a navigation table to help them find the way. The needle in the centre measured the height of the sun. The navigator could move a bar around the notched edge of the table to plot the ship's course.

VIKING SETTLERS on Greenland hunted animals such as reindeer, bears and Arctic hares for meat. They used the skins for clothing and the fur for cloaks. To keep warm in Arctic lands they wore tunics under long-sleeved shirts.

A New Route to Asia

By the 16th century Viking knowledge of the Arctic had been lost, and very little was known about the region. However, European merchants and sailors began to look towards the Arctic for a sailing route, or passage, to China and the East. In the 13th century the explorer Marco Polo had visited the Far East, and returned with tales of fabulous wealth. But Polo's route overland was now blocked by Muslim empires, and the southern sea routes to the East were controlled by Spain and Portugal. England, France and Holland hoped to discover a new route to China via the north-west, beyond the island of Newfoundland (discovered by John Cabot in 1497) or via the north-east, north of Russia.

In 1576 an English expedition led by a captain called Martin Frobisher set off to seek the Northwest Passage. After a stormy crossing the ships reached a deep inlet on Baffin Island in northern Canada, now called Frobisher Bay. The captain believed the inlet was a narrow strait which led to China. In the bay the English spotted "a number of small things fleeting in the sea far off", which they thought must be seals or fish.

In fact they were Inuit in their kayaks (canoes). The Inuit paddled closer and soon surrounded Frobisher's ship. Their facial features confused the English, who took them to be Asians. Frobisher captured an Inuit and took him back to England, together with samples he had found of a strange black rock which glittered like gold. In England it was thought that the rocks contained gold, and Frobisher made two further trips to the region to collect large quantities of the rock.

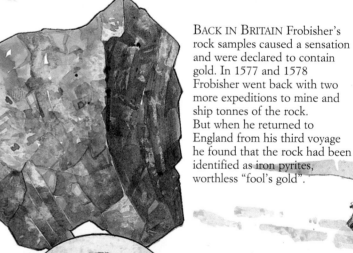

BACK IN BRITAIN Frobisher's rock samples caused a sensation and were declared to contain gold. In 1577 and 1578 Frobisher went back with two more expeditions to mine and ship tonnes of the rock. But when he returned to England from his third voyage he found that the rock had been identified as iron pyrites, worthless "fool's gold".

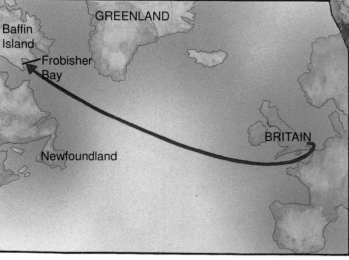

GREENLAND

Baffin Island

Frobisher Bay

Newfoundland

BRITAIN

Route taken by Frobisher on his three voyages to the Arctic, past the southern tip of Greenland to Frobisher Bay on Baffin Island.

MARTIN FROBISHER (1535-1594) was a tough and able commander. But he was disgraced when the "fool's gold" he had collected was found to be worthless, and his claim to have found the route to China was discredited.

THIS EARLY woodcut print (*right*) shows the Inuit with their one-person kayaks on the ice, hunting seals with spears.

The Inuit attack Frobisher's boat.

RELATIONS between Frobisher and the Inuit were uneasy and sometimes hostile. During the first voyage five English sailors were kidnapped by the Inuit. Frobisher captured an Inuit hoping to trade hostages, but the five sailors were never seen again. In England the Inuit soon became ill and died of pneumonia. In 1577 English sailors clashed with Inuits. Spears and bows were no match for the muskets of the sailors.

An Arctic Winter

In the 16th century, explorers also searched the frozen seas north of Scandinavia and Siberia for a north-east route to China. The main rivals were the English and the Dutch. In 1553 the English sent an expedition led by a soldier, Sir Hugh Willoughby. Willoughby was not a seaman but he commanded one ship, and his pilot Richard Chancellor, an expert navigator, another. The ships became separated in a great storm off the coast of Norway. Willoughby's crew managed to land on the Kola Peninsula but starved to death during the winter. Chancellor sailed on to land on the Russian coast at the Dvina River. He travelled 1120 kilometres by sledge to the court of the Russian Tsar in Moscow, and set up trade links with Russia.

In the 1590s the Dutch sent three expeditions to look for the Northeast Passage. They were led by an experienced pilot named Willem Barents. On his first voyage in 1594 Barents reached Novaya Zemlya, a group of islands north of Russia, and entered the icy Kara Sea. In 1595 he tried again, but the ice was worse and he got no further.

In 1596 Barents sailed north to discover the islands of Spitsbergen. The ship then sailed east, but was crushed in the ice north of Novaya Zemlya. Barents and his men were forced to abandon ship and became the first Europeans to survive a winter in the Arctic.

ON THE ROOF of their hut Barents' men built a wooden tower, with the crow's nest from the ship on top, to act as a look-out post. Inside were wooden bunks, a stove and even a kind of bath where each man could wash once a week.

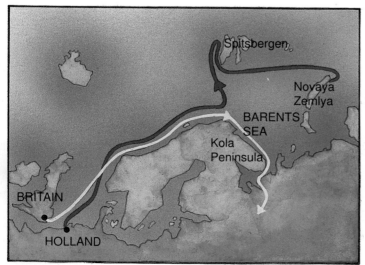

Spitsbergen

Novaya Zemlya

BARENTS SEA

Kola Peninsula

BRITAIN

HOLLAND

Chancellor

Barents 1596

12

The crew salvaged driftwood and built a hut nine metres long and six metres wide. They called it "Ice Haven", and there they passed a long, harsh winter. The following June when the ice began to melt, they escaped in two rowing boats saved from the ship. As they rounded the tip of Novaya Zemlya, Barents took one last look at the "cursed land" and died. The survivors struggled 2560 kilometres across the Barents Sea to the Kola Peninsula where they were rescued.

IN THE 1590S Willem Barents made three voyages to seek the Northeast Passage. He died off the coast of Novaya Zemlya, in the sea that was named after him. The passage was finally sailed by Finnish explorer Baron Nordenskjold in 1878-9.

Polar bears circling "Ice Haven".

DURING the Arctic winter Barents' crew shot polar bears for meat and used the fat to light oil lamps. They gathered driftwood for their fire, which smoked badly inside the hut.

FOR THREE MONTHS, from November to January, the sun never rose above the horizon, and the cold was bitter. Ice formed on the walls of the hut and the sheets froze on the bunks. Wine froze into a solid block and had to be chipped off in chunks. At night the men were disturbed by Arctic foxes running over the roof of "Ice Haven", and when they left the hut during the day they were chased by bears. By the end of winter many of the men were suffering from scurvy, a disease caused by lack of vitamin C, found in fresh fruit and vegetables. Barents was very weak and died soon after they began their escape to the Kola Peninsula.

Mutiny in the Arctic

While the Dutch were exploring the Arctic waters north-east of Scandinavia, English interest in a trade route to China via the north-east or the north-west continued. One of the key figures in the search was Henry Hudson, who led a number of expeditions in the early 1600s. In 1607 and 1608 he made two voyages to the north-eastern Arctic, but was hemmed in by pack ice and forced to turn back. In 1609, working for a Dutch trading group called the East India Company, he set out again. Finding the route eastwards blocked, he crossed the Atlantic to try his luck to the north-west. He reached the site of what is now New York and discovered the wide river now called the Hudson River.

In 1610, sailing this time for England, Hudson headed west in a ship called the *Discovery*. Nearing Newfoundland, he came upon "a great and whirling sea", a channel with swirling tides. Hudson passed through it to enter a bay, now called Hudson Bay.

Hudson's crew were eager to return to England, but convinced that Asia lay on the far side of this "sea", Hudson proceeded to explore the bay. The ship's departure was delayed until the route home was blocked by ice. His crew were forced to spend a terrible winter on the shores of Hudson Bay, while food rations ran short. Among the crew it was rumoured that Hudson kept a secret hoard of food.

The following summer the ice began to break up, but now there was not enough food left for the journey home. This was the last straw for the miserable sailors. In June 1611 they mutinied, taking control of the *Discovery* and setting Hudson adrift in a small boat in the icy waters of the great bay. The tiny boat was never seen again.

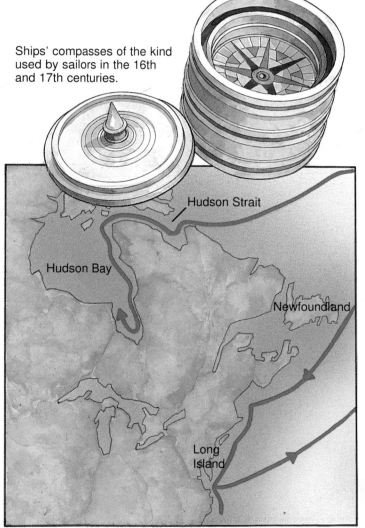

Ships' compasses of the kind used by sailors in the 16th and 17th centuries.

Hudson Strait

Hudson Bay

Newfoundland

Long Island

DESPITE his faults, Henry Hudson was a courageous explorer and a skilful navigator. He came closer to finding the Northwest Passage than previous explorers, but a route to Asia would not be found for another 300 years.

Hudson's routes to North America. On the first voyage he reached Long Island. On the second he discovered Hudson Bay.

THE MUTINEERS cast Hudson adrift in an open boat with his son John and a few loyal sailors. They had no food or weapons. The mutineers searched the captain's cabin and found a great store of ship's biscuits, meal and several kegs of beer. In 1631 the remains of a ruined shelter were found on the shore of Hudson Bay. Some believed that it was built by Hudson and his sailors. After abandoning Hudson the mutineers sailed for England, but some were killed in a fight with Inuit, and others died of starvation. Few survived to reach English shores.

Hudson is cast adrift with his son and five crew members.

15

Exploring Siberia

By the late 17th century, Russia controlled an enormous area of northern Asia as far as Kamchatka on the Pacific Ocean. The empire's northern border in Siberia was unmapped, and no one knew whether or not Asia and America were joined. In 1724 Tsar Peter the Great decided that the territory should be explored. He appointed Vitus Bering, a Danish captain in the Russian navy, to lead the expedition. Bering himself was given the job of discovering if Russia was joined to America. First he had to travel 8000 kilometres across Russia from St. Petersburg to Okhotsk on the Pacific.

In 1727 Bering headed north-east from Okhotsk, and sailed through the narrow strait now named after him. He then returned to St Petersburg.

But the Tsar was not satisfied as Bering had not actually landed in America. In 1741 Bering finally landed on the Alaskan coast. On the return voyage his ship was wrecked on an island off Kamchatka. There, he and his crew passed a terrible winter. Many, including Bering himself, died. Russia's eastern border was mapped, but at great cost.

The task of charting the northern coast of Siberia from the White Sea to the Chukchi peninusula was divided into five great stages. It was carried out by Russian officers and wild frontiersmen called Cossacks, and took ten years to complete.

DURING his second voyage Vitus Bering (1680-1741) sighted Mount Elias, in Alaska, and landed on Kayak Island just off the Alaskan mainland. His task was finished, but the return voyage was plagued by storms and fog. In August 1741 his ship was wrecked on the island now named after him. Worn out by 20 years of Arctic exploration, Bering died of scurvy and exhaustion in December.

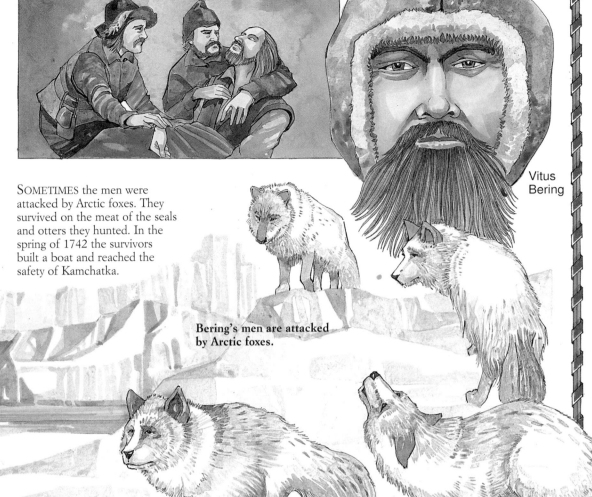

Vitus Bering

DURING the winter of 1741 Bering's men were plagued by disease and hunger. To shelter from the bitter cold they dug holes in the island's sandhills and covered them with the ship's sails.

SOMETIMES the men were attacked by Arctic foxes. They survived on the meat of the seals and otters they hunted. In the spring of 1742 the survivors built a boat and reached the safety of Kamchatka.

Bering's men are attacked by Arctic foxes.

PETER THE GREAT ruled as Tsar of Russia in the early 18th century. During his 26-year reign he strengthened the Russian Empire, partly by ordering unknown parts of Russian territory to be explored and mapped. He selected Vitus Bering to head the task. It was the largest programme of Arctic exploration ever undertaken.

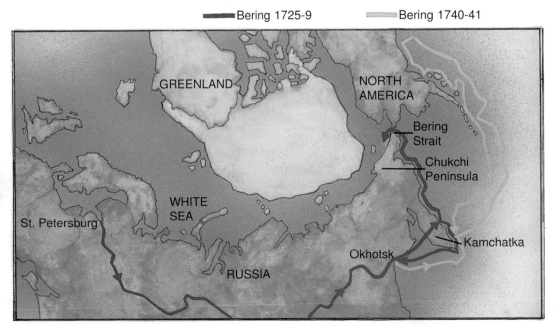

■ Bering 1725-9   Bering 1740-41

GREENLAND

NORTH AMERICA

Bering Strait

Chukchi Peninsula

WHITE SEA

St. Petersburg

Kamchatka

Okhotsk

RUSSIA

The Mystery of the Lost Ships

In the 17th and 18th centuries British ships continued to search for the Northwest Passage. In 1845 an expedition was led by an experienced explorer, Sir John Franklin. Franklin's two ships, *Erebus* and *Terror*, set sail in May 1845, but soon vanished without trace. Their disappearance became one of the great mysteries of the Arctic.

Franklin's ships were stocked with provisions for three years, so at first no one was worried. But in 1848 the British Navy sent a rescue ship. Over the next 14 years many search-parties were mounted – by the navy, by the Hudson's Bay Company (a trading company which had been established in northern Canada), and by Franklin's wife Jane.

The most successful searches were made by Dr John Rae and Leopold McClintock. In 1853 Rae travelled north from Hudson Bay on foot. He heard from the Inuit that 40 Europeans had been seen trudging south. The Inuit showed him cutlery, engraved with Franklin's crest, recovered from two ships abandoned near King William Island. In 1859 search-parties led by McClintock reached King William Island. They found a ship's lifeboat and human skeletons. Further on they found a cairn of stones containing a message from Franklin's crew.

The message explained the fate of the expedition. In 1846 the ships had become trapped in ice off King William Island. They had remained there for two years, during which time Franklin and many men had died of hunger and scurvy. In April 1848, 105 survivors had left to begin the long trek south to Hudson Bay. They had reached the Back River only to die of cold and hunger. It was a terrible story, but the many searches added greatly to knowledge of the Arctic.

Franklin 1845-8

Rae 1853

McClintock 1857-9

FRANKLIN'S SHIPS passed Devon Island and Cornwallis Island. They spent the summer at Beechey Island but by September they were trapped in ice off King William Island.

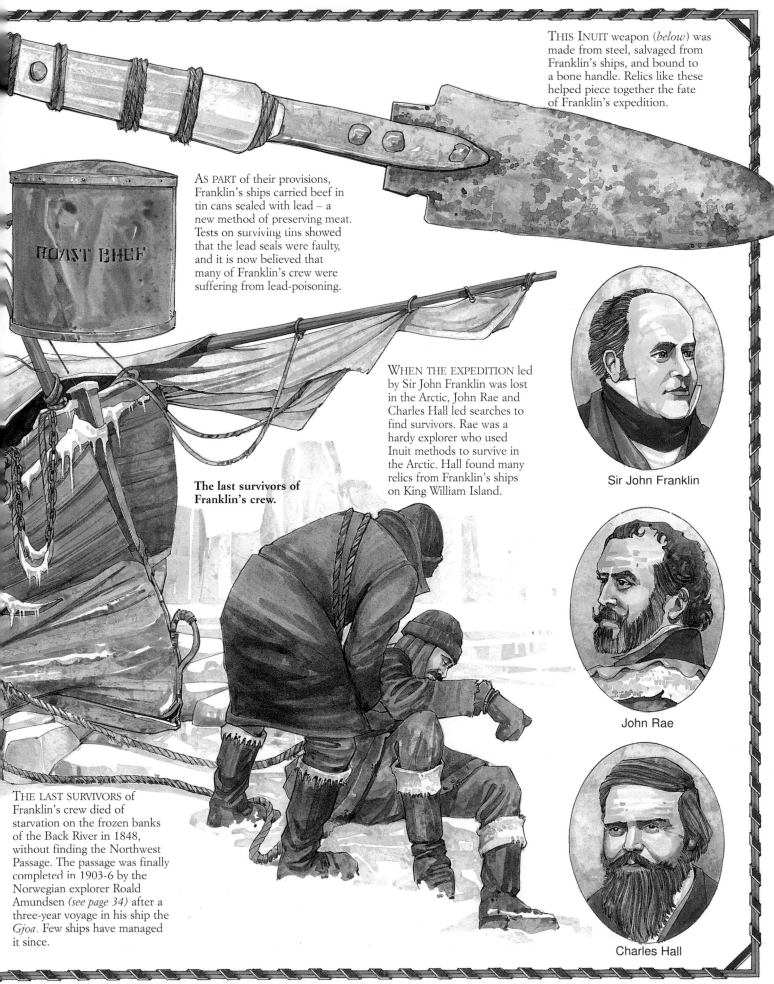

THIS INUIT weapon (*below*) was made from steel, salvaged from Franklin's ships, and bound to a bone handle. Relics like these helped piece together the fate of Franklin's expedition.

AS PART of their provisions, Franklin's ships carried beef in tin cans sealed with lead – a new method of preserving meat. Tests on surviving tins showed that the lead seals were faulty, and it is now believed that many of Franklin's crew were suffering from lead-poisoning.

ROAST BEEF

The last survivors of Franklin's crew.

WHEN THE EXPEDITION led by Sir John Franklin was lost in the Arctic, John Rae and Charles Hall led searches to find survivors. Rae was a hardy explorer who used Inuit methods to survive in the Arctic. Hall found many relics from Franklin's ships on King William Island.

Sir John Franklin

John Rae

Charles Hall

THE LAST SURVIVORS of Franklin's crew died of starvation on the frozen banks of the Back River in 1848, without finding the Northwest Passage. The passage was finally completed in 1903-6 by the Norwegian explorer Roald Amundsen (*see page 34*) after a three-year voyage in his ship the *Gjoa*. Few ships have managed it since.

Drifting to the Pole

In 1881 one disaster in the Arctic led to another great expedition. The American ship *Jeannette* was crushed by ice north of Siberia. Three years later, remains from the ship were washed up in Greenland, having drifted 4800 kilometres in the ice. This find gave Norwegian Fridtjof Nansen the idea of drifting in the ice to the North Pole. Nansen had a special ship built for the journey, which would ride high in the ice rather than be crushed by it. He named it *Fram*, meaning "forward".

In June 1893 Nansen set off in the *Fram* with 13 crew. The ship sped east and north, and was locked in the ice by September. For two winters the ship drifted slowly, but by 1895 Nansen realized they would miss the Pole. He resolved to make his own way there by sledge and kayak, and chose an officer, Hjalmar Johansen, to go with him.

The two set out in March. At first they made progress north, but soon ice ridges barred the way. Only 386 kilometres from the Pole, Nansen gave up and struggled south again. In August they reached Franz Josef Land. Another Arctic winter was arriving, so they built a stone hut and passed the winter there. The following May they headed south again. Camped on another island, they heard barking and saw a dog, and then a man. Nansen ran to meet the stranger, who turned out to be Frederick Jackson, an English explorer. In Jackson's ship they sailed home to Norway, where Nansen became a hero. A week later the *Fram* returned too.

FRIDTJOF NANSEN (1861-1930) was convinced, by the story of the *Jeannette*, that under the polar ice sheet was a great ocean with powerful currents. Riding on this vast ice raft, Nansen believed a ship might reach the Pole. After his voyage he became a statesman and was awarded the Nobel Peace Prize in 1922.

THE *FRAM* drifted in the ice for three years. But by 1895 Nansen realized the ship had drifted too far westwards. It was obvious it would miss his goal, the North Pole itself.

━━ Drifting of the *Fram*

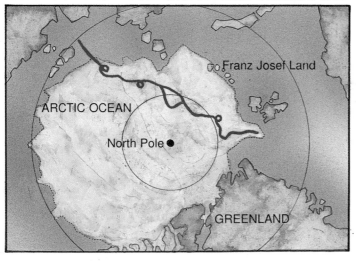

Franz Josef Land

ARCTIC OCEAN

North Pole ●

GREENLAND

The *Fram*

Nansen and Johansen begin
their dash to the North Pole.

THE *FRAM* was specially built
for drifting in the ice, with
sloping sides to withstand the
pressure of pack ice. A windmill
provided electricity. In March
1895 Nansen and Johansen left
for the Pole with dogs and
kayaks. A month later they
turned back, but they had little
food left. The men were forced
to kill the dogs for meat and
pull the sledges themselves.
When the ice melted, they
lashed the kayaks together and
rigged a sail. Once Nansen's
canoe was ripped by a walrus's
tusk and nearly sank. Another
time while the men camped on
the ice, the kayaks drifted away.
Nansen plunged into the icy
waters and nearly drowned
trying to save them.

The Pole at Last

By 1900 a number of explorers had tried to reach the North Pole. None had succeeded and some had died in the attempt. But Robert Peary, a young officer in the United States Navy, was determined to make his name by getting there first. Peary made a total of eight trips to the Arctic. In the 1880s and 1890s he led expeditions to the Pole from northern Greenland, and proved that Greenland was an island, not part of the Arctic continent. Each time, Peary got closer to the Pole before being forced to turn back.

In July 1908 he set off again for the Pole, in the *Roosevelt*, a special steam-powered ship designed to break through the ice. With him was Matthew Henson, the friend who had worked for him for 20 years. The expedition set out from Cape Columbia on Ellesmere Island. Peary had hired 50 Inuit and 250 dogs to help them, and planned to use Inuit methods to reach the Pole. The men dressed in sealskins and camped in igloos, Inuit snow-houses.

Inuit support teams led the way northwards for two months. Then Peary, Henson and four Inuit with 40 dogs took over with 214 kilometres to go. On 7 April 1909, after five long marches, they reached their goal. "The Pole at last!!! The prize of three centuries, my dream and ambition for 23 years," wrote Peary in his diary. The men built an igloo camp and Peary planted the American flag, sewn by his wife, at the top of the world.

Compass used by Peary on his trip to the North Pole.

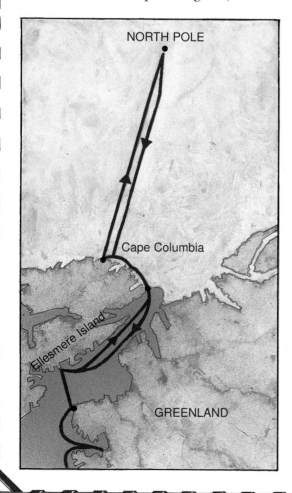

NORTH POLE

Cape Columbia

Ellesmere Island

GREENLAND

—— Route of Peary's ship

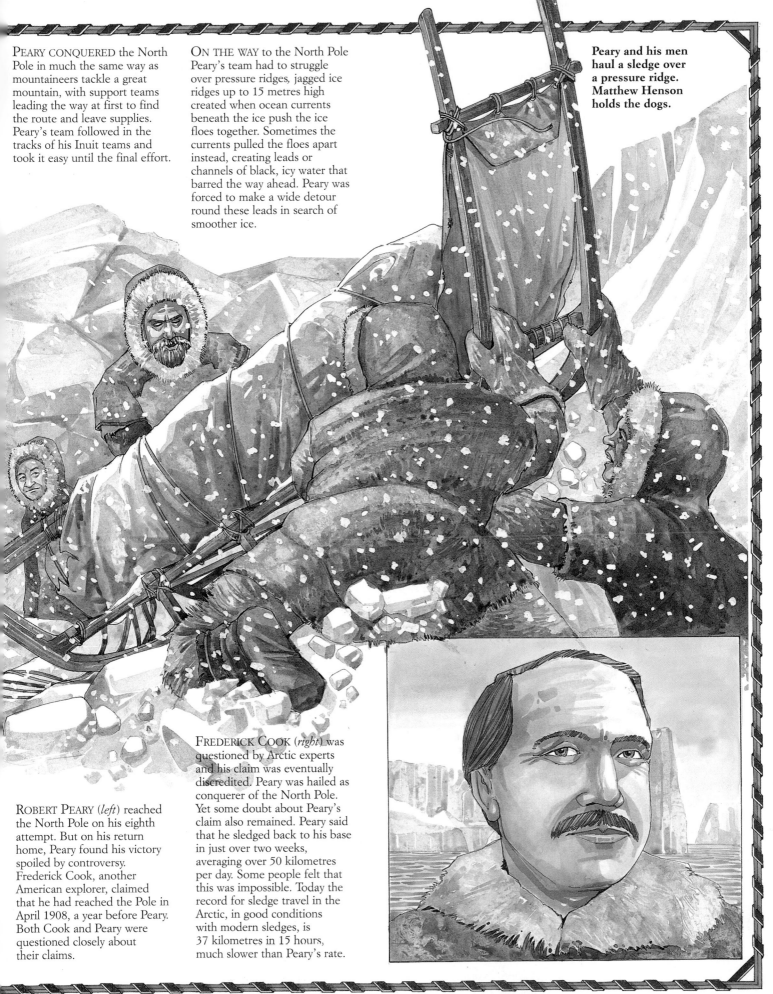

PEARY CONQUERED the North Pole in much the same way as mountaineers tackle a great mountain, with support teams leading the way at first to find the route and leave supplies. Peary's team followed in the tracks of his Inuit teams and took it easy until the final effort.

ON THE WAY to the North Pole Peary's team had to struggle over pressure ridges, jagged ice ridges up to 15 metres high created when ocean currents beneath the ice push the ice floes together. Sometimes the currents pulled the floes apart instead, creating leads or channels of black, icy water that barred the way ahead. Peary was forced to make a wide detour round these leads in search of smoother ice.

Peary and his men haul a sledge over a pressure ridge. Matthew Henson holds the dogs.

ROBERT PEARY (*left*) reached the North Pole on his eighth attempt. But on his return home, Peary found his victory spoiled by controversy. Frederick Cook, another American explorer, claimed that he had reached the Pole in April 1908, a year before Peary. Both Cook and Peary were questioned closely about their claims.

FREDERICK COOK (*right*) was questioned by Arctic experts and his claim was eventually discredited. Peary was hailed as conquerer of the North Pole. Yet some doubt about Peary's claim also remained. Peary said that he sledged back to his base in just over two weeks, averaging over 50 kilometres per day. Some people felt that this was impossible. Today the record for sledge travel in the Arctic, in good conditions with modern sledges, is 37 kilometres in 15 hours, much slower than Peary's rate.

Living with the Inuit

Peary achieved success in the Arctic partly by using Inuit methods. But the greatest expert on the Inuit way of life was Vilhjalmur Stefansson, a Canadian explorer who lived among Inuit peoples for many years. He made his first trip to the Arctic in 1906. He planned to study the Inuit and arranged to join an expedition at Herschel Island near Mackenzie Bay in northern Canada. The expedition ship carried all his gear and Arctic clothing. Stefansson reached Herschel Island overland, dressed in lightweight summer clothes. But when the ship did not arrive he was not worried. From October to the following March he lived with the Inuit of Mackenzie Bay, and studied their customs and traditions.

In May 1907 he returned to Herschel Island. This time he had all the equipment needed for his new expedition except matches. He trekked north-west to Point Barrow for matches, and spent the winter there, making friends with two Inuit called Natkusiak and Tannaumirk. In the spring they travelled east and met the Inuit of Victoria Island. They were very friendly and built a special igloo for their guests. Stefansson stayed with them for a year, finding out about their way of life.

D∪RING HIS TIME at Mackenzie Bay and Victoria Island, Stefansson lived as the Inuit did, wearing their style of clothes, and sharing their food. He learned their languages and studied how they survived the harsh Arctic conditions. He learned how to build an igloo and how to hunt seals. Seal-hunters crawled towards their prey over the ice, pretending to be seals until they were close enough to spear the animals.

T∪E VICTORIA ISLAND Inuit told Stefansson of Inuit with blond hair, who lived to the North. He found the group and named them the Copper Eskimos because they made tools from copper. Stefansson was interested in their fair hair. He guessed that they were descended either from the crew of Franklin's ship (*see page 18*) or from the Vikings who had reached Greenland 900 years before. These ideas caused much discussion when Stefansson returned home.

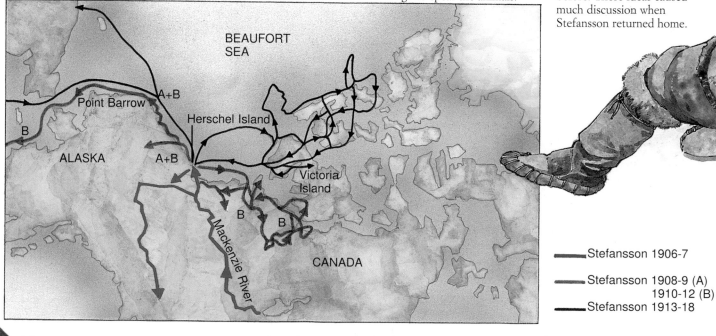

BEAUFORT SEA

A+B

Point Barrow

B

Herschel Island

ALASKA

A+B

Victoria Island

B

B

Mackenzie River

CANADA

— Stefansson 1906-7

— Stefansson 1908-9 (A) 1910-12 (B)

— Stefansson 1913-18

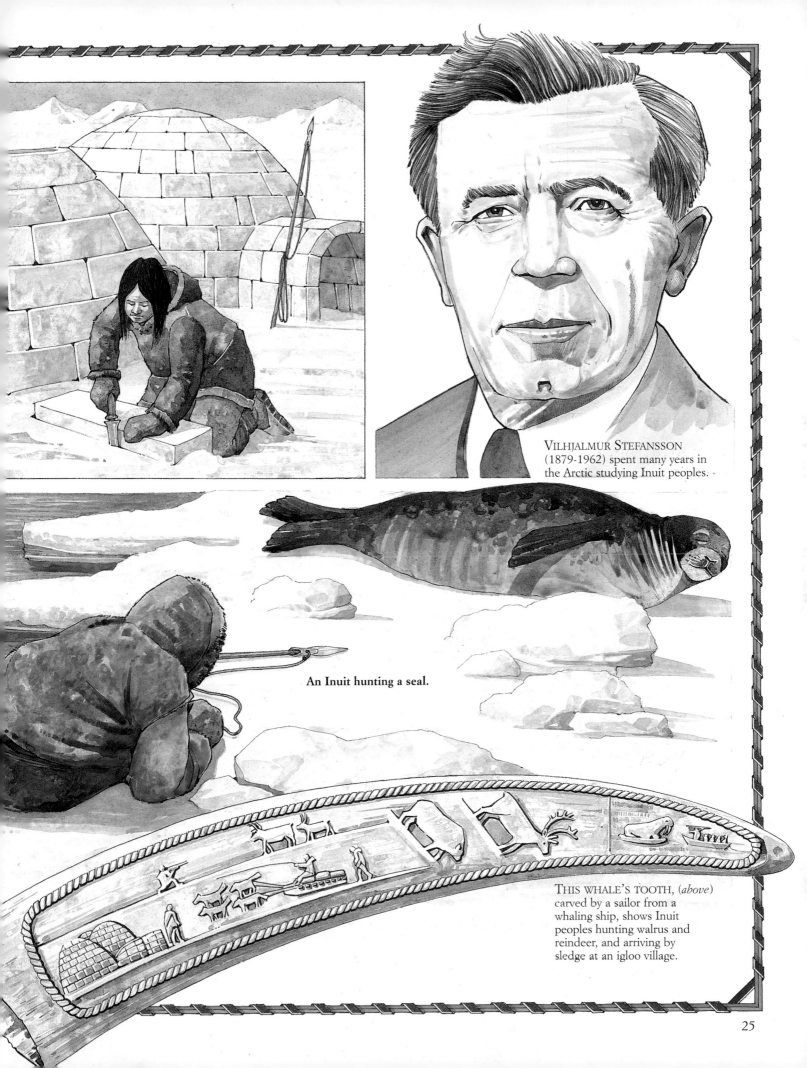

VILHJALMUR STEFANSSON (1879-1962) spent many years in the Arctic studying Inuit peoples.

An Inuit hunting a seal.

THIS WHALE'S TOOTH, (*above*) carved by a sailor from a whaling ship, shows Inuit peoples hunting walrus and reindeer, and arriving by sledge at an igloo village.

The Last Great Arctic Journey

Robert Peary's conquest of the North Pole ended the great age of Arctic exploration. Soon, more modern machinery replaced traditional dog teams in the Arctic. Aeroplanes flew over the North Pole and in 1958 a submarine, the *Nautilus*, passed beneath it. Yet one Arctic challenge remained – to cross the frozen Arctic Ocean, via the Pole itself. In the late 1960s this challenge was taken up by a British team, led by Wally Herbert.

Herbert planned to leave Alaska in spring 1968. The party would use traditional sledges pulled by dog teams, but would depend on supplies dropped by aircraft along the route. They would camp on the ice in summer when the ice was too soft to make progress, sledge on in the autumn and camp again for the winter, when it would be too dark and cold to travel. Meanwhile the drift of the ice would carry them nearer to their goal. Herbert planned to race for Spitsbergen the following spring.

In February 1968 the party set out, but ice ridges and leads of open water made progress very slow. By the time they made camp in summer on a large ice floe, they were well behind schedule. In the autumn they had made only a little progress when one of the team, Allan Gill, badly injured his back. The team were forced to turn back and sit out the long, dark winter at their old summer camp-site while he recovered. The following February the team set out again, reaching the North Pole on 6 April 1969. Heading south for Spitsbergen they made faster progress, but now the expedition had become a race against time. They had to reach the safety of land before the pack ice melted under their feet. On 23 May they saw land at last, passed one more night on a tiny ice floe and then rushed across the melting slush to reach firm ground. The last great Arctic journey had ended in success.

WALLY HERBERT travelled from Point Barrow in Alaska, via the North Pole to the islands of Spitsbergen in the Barents Sea, a distance of 5920 kilometres.

—— The route of Wally Herbert's Arctic crossing.

DURING THE ARCTIC CROSSING Herbert's team spent 18 months on shifting ice floes less than two metres thick. The floes threatened to split beneath their feet at any time, plunging them into the freezing waters below. On one occasion Ken Hedges, a team member, nearly lost his sledge and dogs when a wide lead opened in the ice. At night they feared the pack ice would split beneath their tents. Several times they were chased by polar bears, and once a stove fell over and set one of the tents on fire.

Ken Hedges rescues his dog team.

WALLY HERBERT was born in 1934. As a boy he dreamed of crossing the Arctic, and as a young man he gained experience of polar regions in the Antarctic. In 1964 he began to raise money and support for his expedition, but it took four years to gain the funds to go ahead.

Wally Herbert

The Search for the Antarctic

By the late 18th century most of the world had been explored and mapped. But Antarctica, bordered by ice-choked, foggy seas had still not been discovered. Yet rumours of a great southern land persisted. In 1772 the British government sent the explorer Captain James Cook to find it. In three voyages Cook's ships crossed the Antarctic Circle and sailed around Antarctica without sighting land. Turning north, Cook discovered the island of South Georgia. It was home to many seals and penguins, and its coastal waters were teeming with whales. His reports brought the ships of seal- and whale-hunters south to Antarctic waters, and it was these sailors who first saw land.

The Antarctic Peninsula stretches 1600 kilometres north towards Cape Horn at the tip of South America. It was here, in 1819-20, that two British sailors, William Smith and Edward Bransfield, discovered the South Shetland Islands and sighted the Antarctic mainland to the east. The same year an American sealer, Nathaniel Palmer, climbed the mountains of Deception Island in the South Shetlands and saw "an extensive mountain country heavily laden with ice and snow". But other countries were also interested in the unknown continent. One night Palmer anchored in uncharted Antarctic waters in thick fog. In the morning when the fog lifted Palmer found his little ship between two huge Russian vessels. The ships were commanded by Captain von Bellingshausen, who had sailed around Antarctica without realizing that the great mountains and ice cliffs he saw were land.

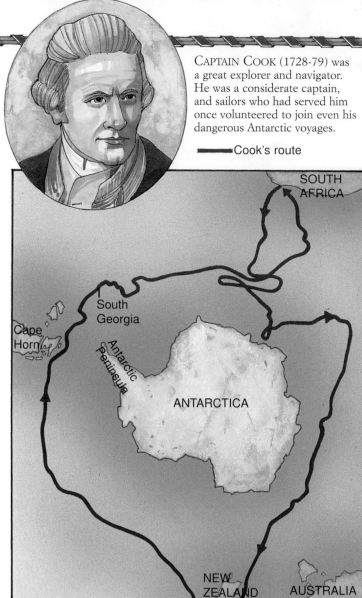

CAPTAIN COOK (1728-79) was a great explorer and navigator. He was a considerate captain, and sailors who had served him once volunteered to join even his dangerous Antarctic voyages.

— Cook's route

SOUTH AFRICA

South Georgia

Cape Horn

Antarctic Peninsula

ANTARCTICA

NEW ZEALAND

AUSTRALIA

FOR HIS ANTARCTIC expeditions between 1773-5 Cook's ships were the *Resolution* and the *Adventure*. He sailed right around the continent but found his way south barred by ice.

ON LONG whaling voyages sailors spent their spare time carving pictures on whales' teeth. The carvings, called scrimshaw, were made with heavy sailcloth needles.

Scrimshaw

IN 1821 an American seal-hunter called John Davis was the first to send men ashore on the continent of Antarctica. The crew landed at Hughes Bay, south of Deception Island. They found no seals, but a "high land covered entirely with snow". Heading north again, Davis wrote "I think this Southern Land to be a Continent."

In 1823 an English sealer named James Weddell made another important discovery whilst cruising the polar seas further east in search of seals. He broke through the ice-choked waters to sail far south into a vast bay now called the Weddell Sea.

Davis's crew land on Antarctica.

29

A New Continent

Dumont d'Urville   Ross   Wilkes

Between 1830 and 1850 exploration in the Antarctic became a race to reach the magnetic South Pole. For years sailors had used magnetic compasses to navigate. But now the use of faster, steam-powered ships led to a need for more accurate compasses, and to an interest in the magnetic poles. In 1831 an English explorer, James Clark Ross, discovered the magnetic North Pole on the Boothia Peninsula, about 1600 kilometres from the geographic pole (*see map on page 18*). Now Britain, France and the United States struggled to be first to reach the magnetic South Pole.

The French ships, led by Dumont d'Urville, sailed in 1837, followed in 1838 by an American fleet commanded by Charles Wilkes. Both expeditions were poorly equipped. The French fleet had been prepared for a voyage to the tropics, not Antarctica.

The Americans sent warships, with large gunports through which icy water poured, flooding the decks. The British expedition, led by Ross himself, set sail in 1839. His two ships, *Erebus* and *Terror*, were small but sturdily built. The same ships would be used by Sir John Franklin on his ill-fated voyage to the Arctic (*see page 18*).

The French and the Americans made the first official sightings of Antarctica on the same day, 18 January 1840. Dumont d'Urville discovered a snow-covered land with towering cliffs which he named Adélie Land, after his wife. He sent a small boat ashore to plant the French flag, alarming a colony of penguins nesting there, which d'Urville named Adélie penguins. Wilkes' ships mapped 2400 kilometres of coastline.

Aware that the French and the Americans were in the area, Ross tried his luck further east. In January 1841 *Erebus* and *Terror* battled past icebergs in the South Pacific Ocean to reach the clear waters of a huge bay now called the Ross Sea. Ross sailed on south in search of the magnetic Pole, to reach a rocky land with soaring mountains and great glaciers. He named his discovery Victoria Land after the young British queen, Victoria, who had been crowned in 1837.

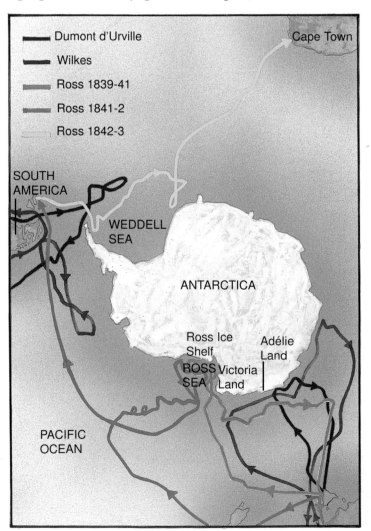

Dumont d'Urville
Wilkes
Ross 1839-41
Ross 1841-2
Ross 1842-3

Cape Town

SOUTH AMERICA

WEDDELL SEA

ANTARCTICA

Ross Ice Shelf

Adélie Land

ROSS SEA

Victoria Land

PACIFIC OCEAN

JULES DUMONT D'URVILLE was an officer in the French Navy. He sighted Antarctica only ten hours after Charles Wilkes. Wilkes was a very strict captain. On his return he was court-martialled for the cruel treatment of his crew. James Clark Ross had many years' experience in the Arctic before sailing for Antarctica.

Ross sails past the active volcano Mount Erebus.

SAILING SOUTH in the Ross Sea in January 1841, Ross saw a mountainous island with a peak 3760 metres high, spouting smoke and flames. Ross named this active volcano Mount Erebus after his ship, and a smaller, inactive volcano Mount Terror. Sailing on they came upon an even more incredible sight – a white line stretching across the horizon. As they sailed closer they saw it was an ice cliff 60 metres high, now known as the Ross Ice Shelf.

THE ROSS ICE SHELF is a vast slab of floating ice larger in size than France. For Ross it barred the way towards the magnetic South Pole. "We might with equal chance of success try to sail through the cliffs of Dover," he wrote. The ships spent two more summers (December-February in Antarctica) without getting any further south.

Early Antarctic Exploration

In the late 1800s and early 1900s explorers continued to visit Antarctica, so the coastline was mapped and claimed by different countries. In 1894 an Australian expedition was first to spend a winter in Antarctica. One of the great explorers was Douglas Mawson (1882-1958), an English scientist whose family emigrated to Australia when he was a boy. In 1908, on an expedition led by Ernest Shackleton (*see page 38*), Mawson climbed Mount Erebus and reached the magnetic South Pole.

In 1911 Mawson led an Australian expedition to survey the coast near Adélie Land. He established his base at Commonwealth Bay, while his ship the *Aurora* took a team, led by Englishman Frank Wild, to explore further west. Weather conditions were so bad Mawson called his base "The Home of the Blizzard". His team of scientists battled on hands and knees through winds of up to 300 kph, to take their measurements a short distance from the hut.

In November 1912 Mawson set out on a sledging expedition with two companions, a British army officer named B.E.S. Ninnis and Xavier Mertz, a Swiss skiing champion. The party had been away a month when disaster struck. An ice bridge over a crevasse gave way and Ninnis fell in, along with a sledge and most of their supplies.

Mawson and Mertz were stranded 480 kilometres from safety with only 10 days' supply of food. Soon they had to kill their dogs for meat and pull the sledges themselves. On 1 January 1913 Mertz collapsed, and died a week later. Starving and with 160 kilometres to go, Mawson struggled on alone. Still 45 kilometres from safety he found a cairn containing food left by his party. He fought through blizzards and reached his base at last on 1 February. But looking up, he saw the *Aurora* steaming into the distance!

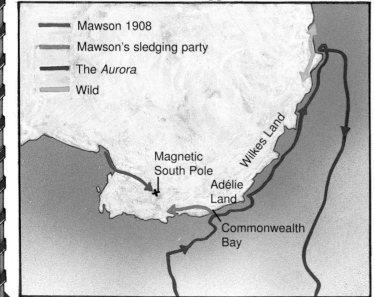

Mawson 1908
Mawson's sledging party
The *Aurora*
Wild

Wilkes Land

Magnetic South Pole

Adélie Land

Commonwealth Bay

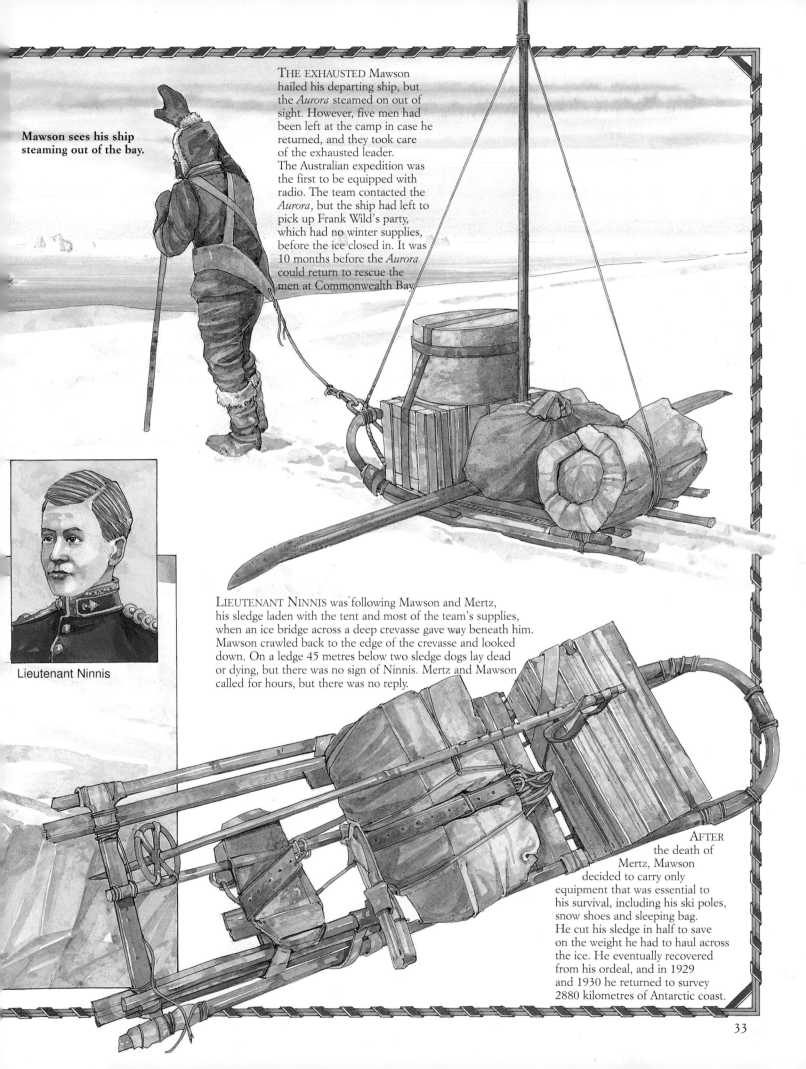

Mawson sees his ship steaming out of the bay.

THE EXHAUSTED Mawson hailed his departing ship, but the *Aurora* steamed on out of sight. However, five men had been left at the camp in case he returned, and they took care of the exhausted leader. The Australian expedition was the first to be equipped with radio. The team contacted the *Aurora*, but the ship had left to pick up Frank Wild's party, which had no winter supplies, before the ice closed in. It was 10 months before the *Aurora* could return to rescue the men at Commonwealth Bay.

Lieutenant Ninnis

LIEUTENANT NINNIS was following Mawson and Mertz, his sledge laden with the tent and most of the team's supplies, when an ice bridge across a deep crevasse gave way beneath him. Mawson crawled back to the edge of the crevasse and looked down. On a ledge 45 metres below two sledge dogs lay dead or dying, but there was no sign of Ninnis. Mertz and Mawson called for hours, but there was no reply.

AFTER the death of Mertz, Mawson decided to carry only equipment that was essential to his survival, including his ski poles, snow shoes and sleeping bag. He cut his sledge in half to save on the weight he had to haul across the ice. He eventually recovered from his ordeal, and in 1929 and 1930 he returned to survey 2880 kilometres of Antarctic coast.

Race for the Pole

In 1910 a race began for the geographic South Pole. In 1902 a British expedition led by Captain Robert Scott had been in Antarctica, and a party with Scott and Ernest Shackleton got within 920 kilometres of the Pole. In 1908 Shackleton reached a point 155 kilometres from the Pole but turned back due to lack of food. In 1909 Scott planned another expedition to reach the Pole. He left Britain for Antarctica in June 1910 with a team of 53 men.

But another explorer was setting his sights on the South Pole. Roald Amundsen was a Norwegian with many years' experience in polar regions. During 1903-6 he became the first to sail the Northwest Passage. From boyhood he had wanted to be first to the North Pole. In 1909 he was ready to set out in Nansen's old ship, the *Fram,* when he heard the news that Peary had already reached the North Pole. He decided to try for the South Pole instead. In a telegram he told Scott of his new goal. "Beg leave to inform you proceeding Antarctica," Scott read to his dismay. The race for the Pole was on.

Scott set up his base at McMurdo Sound on the Ross Ice Shelf on 4 January 1911. He planned to make for the Pole across the ice shelf, climbing the 3030-metre mountain barrier at its end to reach the polar plateau via the Beardmore Glacier as Shackleton had done. On 14 January Amundsen landed further east at the Bay of Whales. His base was nearly 100 kilometres nearer the South Pole, but he would have to pioneer a route to the plateau to reach it.

ROBERT FALCON SCOTT (1868-1912) was a moody and determined British naval officer. He spent years in Antarctica and felt the South Pole was his by right. His ship was an old whaler called the *Terra Nova*, meaning "New Land".

The *Terra Nova*

ROALD AMUNDSEN (1872-1928) dedicated his life to polar exploration. In the Arctic he learned much from the Inuit about travelling and surviving in polar regions. He put this knowledge to good use in the Antarctic.

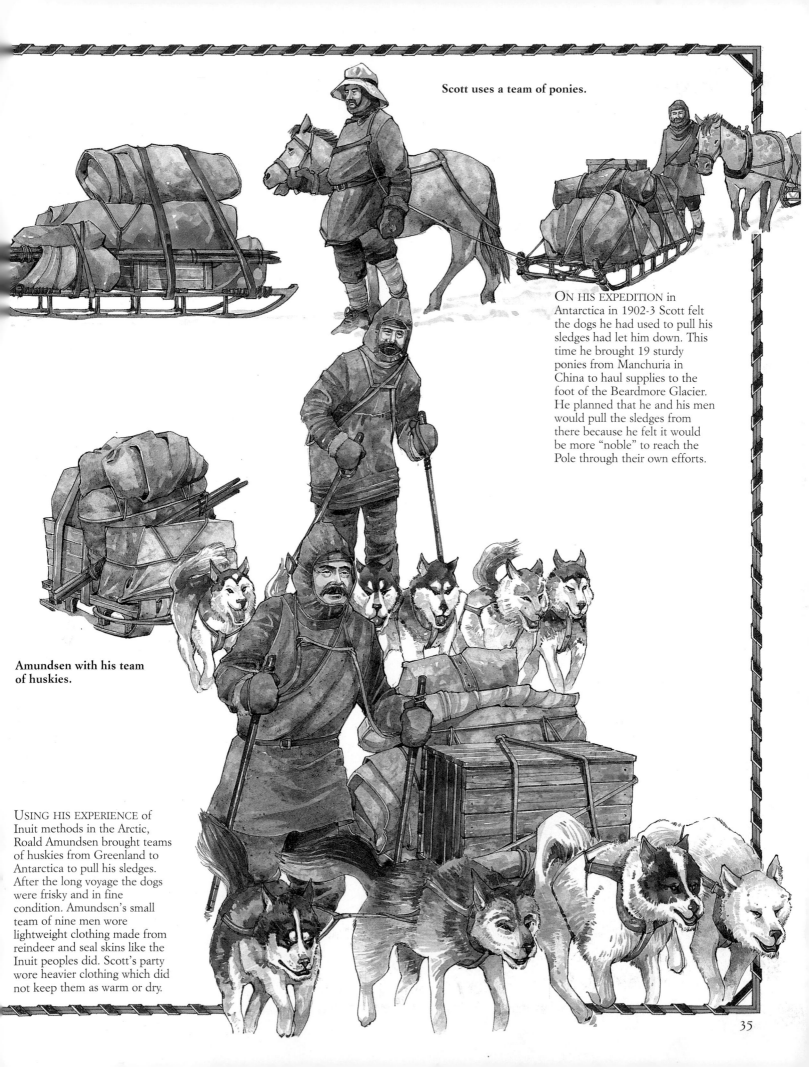

Scott uses a team of ponies.

ON HIS EXPEDITION in Antarctica in 1902-3 Scott felt the dogs he had used to pull his sledges had let him down. This time he brought 19 sturdy ponies from Manchuria in China to haul supplies to the foot of the Beardmore Glacier. He planned that he and his men would pull the sledges from there because he felt it would be more "noble" to reach the Pole through their own efforts.

Amundsen with his team of huskies.

USING HIS EXPERIENCE of Inuit methods in the Arctic, Roald Amundsen brought teams of huskies from Greenland to Antarctica to pull his sledges. After the long voyage the dogs were frisky and in fine condition. Amundsen's small team of nine men wore lightweight clothing made from reindeer and seal skins like the Inuit peoples did. Scott's party wore heavier clothing which did not keep them as warm or dry.

35

Triumph and Disaster

Amundsen set out for the South Pole with four men on 19 October 1911. Scott left with a team of 16 men on 1 November. From the start the Norwegians made good progress, laying supply camps across the Ross Ice Shelf. The huskies pulled well, and sometimes the men let the dogs pull them along, too. Scott's team moved more slowly, laying supplies and making scientific observations. On 15 November they arrived at One Ton Depot, a big supply camp. The ponies were suffering from the cold. Some died, and on 9 December, after a blizzard, the rest had to be shot. From then on Scott's team had to haul the supplies themselves.

Amundsen's team reached the edge of the Ross Ice Shelf by 17 November and forced a route up the narrow Axel Heiberg Glacier.

With plenty of supplies they sledged for the Pole, and reached their goal on 14 December 1911. They planted the Norwegian flag and spent three days there before starting back. Scott's team started up the wider Beardmore Glacier on 10 December, and reached the polar plateau by Christmas. Meanwhile Amundsen was making good time on his way back. He reached his base at the Bay of Whales on 25 January 1912, on the exact day he had planned.

For Scott the agony was just beginning. On 18 January he reached the Pole with a team of four to find the Norwegian flag. It was a bitter disappointment. "Great God! This is an awful place," he wrote in his diary. "Now for the run home and a desperate struggle. I wonder if we can do it?"

- ●   Supply camp
- ▬▬ Admundsen 1911-12
- ▬▬ Scott 1911-12
- ▬▬ Shackleton 1908-9

SCOTT planned to reach the Pole with a team of three men, but at the last minute he took a fourth as well. With an extra man the tent was overcrowded and food rations were short.

REACHING THE SOUTH POLE on 14 December 1911, the Norwegians (*below left*) took photographs and flew their country's flag. The British party (*right*) arrived on 18 January. They were deeply disappointed not to get there first. The next day they started back, but they were plagued by blizzards and were desperately tired. A sailor called Evans was the first man to weaken. As they descended the Beardmore Glacier in February he fell twice, hurting his head. He died soon after.

BY MID-MARCH, as Scott's team struggled back over the Ross Ice Shelf, another man, Captain Oates, became exhausted. Believing he was holding up the party, he left the tent, wandered out into the blizzard and died. But his heroic sacrifice did not save the remaining three. They died of hunger, frost-bite and exhaustion, in late March, in their tent, while a blizzard raged outside. They were only 18 kilometres from their supply camp. Their bodies were found by a search party eight months later, with the diaries that recorded the last days of their terrible journey.

Oates' heroic walk.

SCOTT'S PONIES proved to be unsuitable for the Antarctic. After they were shot, the team had to haul their sledges themselves. This back-breaking work was totally exhausting.

Voyage of Endurance

In 1912, the explorer Ernest Shackleton devised the daring plan of crossing Antarctica via the South Pole. He would need two ships: one would sail to the Weddell Sea, from where Shackleton's party would set out; the other would sail to the Ross Ice Shelf on the opposite side of Antarctica and lay supplies to meet them. The supply ship was Mawson's old boat, *Aurora*. Shackleton's ship was named *Endurance*, after his family motto. He set sail from England in August 1914.

The *Endurance* reached the island of South Georgia in December, but by January 1915 it was caught in the ice of the Weddell Sea. In October it broke up and sank. Shackleton decided to make for the safety of Elephant Island, 160 kilometres away, in the ship's three lifeboats. It was the beginning of an epic journey.

—— The *Endurance*

▬▬ Open boat journey

The boats were jostled by icebergs and the men were tortured by thirst. In April 1916 they reached Elephant Island. But the island was a barren rock where no one would think of looking for them. Shackleton knew he had to reach the whaling station on South Georgia, 1400 kilometres away.

Leaving his crew in the charge of Frank Wild, Shackleton set out in the stoutest boat with five men. They endured terrible storms and raging thirst before reaching South Georgia 14 days later. Even then, the whaling station lay on the far side of the island 240 kilometres away. With two companions, Shackleton scaled the mountains and glaciers of South Georgia to reach the station, and returned with a rescue party to save his crew.

ERNEST SHACKLETON (1874-1922) was known as "the Irish giant". To his devoted men he was just "the Boss". One called him "the greatest leader that ever came on God's earth, bar none".

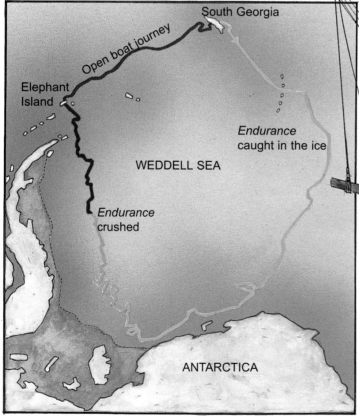

South Georgia

Open boat journey

Elephant Island

Endurance caught in the ice

WEDDELL SEA

Endurance crushed

ANTARCTICA

The *Endurance*

SAILING FROM Elephant Island to South Georgia, Shackleton's tiny boat faced the stormiest seas in the world. It was lashed by gales and battered by waves 15 metres high. Spray froze to the rigging and threatened to capsize the boat. One night Shackleton saw what he thought was a line of clear sky between high clouds. Then he realized it was the white crest of a giant wave rushing down on them. The men held on, though the ship was drenched and nearly sank. They bailed out water furiously and eventually the boat righted itself.

Shackleton and his men brave stormy seas.

IN JANUARY 1915 the pack ice of the Weddell Sea closed around the *Endurance*. The ship never broke free again, although Shackleton and his men spent 10 months camped on the ship. In October the *Endurance* was destroyed by the pack ice.

Exploring Antarctica by Air

In 1921 Shackleton returned to Antarctica for another expedition. But off South Georgia he suffered a heart attack and died. In 1926 Amundsen flew over the North Pole in an airship, becoming the first man to reach both Poles. But in 1928 he died in the Arctic while trying to rescue the crew of another airship which had crashed. The deaths of Shackleton and Amundsen marked the end of the age of heroic exploration in Antarctica. The age of exploration by machines, particularly the aeroplane, had begun.

In 1928 Australian explorer Hubert Wilkins was first to fly an aeroplane over Antarctica. In 1929 Commander Richard Byrd of the United States Navy flew to the South Pole from his base, "Little America" at the Bay of Whales. Byrd cleared the 3030-metre mountain range at the edge of the Ross Ice Shelf with only 150 metres to spare.

In 1933 Byrd went on a scientific expedition. He spent five winter months 200 kilometres from his base in an isolated, draughty weather hut. Its stove was faulty and leaked carbon-monoxide gas. Byrd was slowly being poisoned, but did not want to radio for help and risk the lives of those who would be sent to rescue him. His radio messages became incoherent and a rescue party set out, taking a month to reach the hut. When they arrived Byrd could hardly move, and it was two months before he was well enough to travel.

Byrd takes a scientific measurement

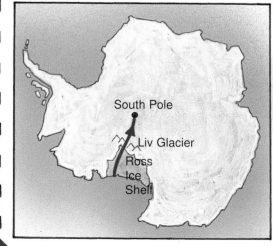

South Pole

Liv Glacier

Ross Ice Shelf

— Byrd's route to the South Pole

Byrd clears the Liv Glacier.

ON HIS FLIGHT to the South Pole in 1929, with a crew of three, Byrd had to scale the 3030-metre mountain barrier to reach the polar plateau. With engines at full throttle the heavily laden plane soared up the unexplored Liv Glacier. Suddenly it refused to climb or respond to the controls. Byrd's crew threw heavy food bags from the plane, and it began to climb again. As the walls of the glacier narrowed Byrd knew they could not turn back. They jettisoned another bag and the plane cleared the glacier with only 150 metres to spare.

COMMANDER RICHARD BYRD (1888-1957) made the first flight over the North Pole in 1926. From 1928-57 he led many scientific expeditions in Antarctica. In 1946-7 he led "Operation Highjump", an ambitious project involving 4700 men, 23 aircraft and 13 ships. It discovered new mountain ranges, 26 new islands and mapped 2240 kilometres of coast.

FOR HIS 2700-kilometre round trip to the South Pole in 1929, Byrd's plane was a primitive Ford Trimotor called the *Floyd Bennett*. It had high wings, and skis for landing on ice or snow.

41

Crossing Antarctica

In 1957, 12 nations set up 50 bases in Antarctica to carry out a programme of scientific study. Dr Vivian Fuchs headed the British team. He planned to cross the continent via the South Pole, fulfilling Ernest Shackleton's dream of 40 years before. Fuchs planned to set out from the Weddell Sea and pass the Pole to reach a series of supply camps that would be laid from the Ross Ice Shelf. His plan was the same as Shackleton's, but the equipment that was available was very different. Fuchs had aeroplanes to scout out the route and drop supplies, motor-driven tractors and a powerful ship, called an ice-breaker, which could crash through the ice floes.

The famous mountaineer Edmund Hillary headed the team laying supplies from the Ross Ice Shelf. By November 1957 the two parties had set out from opposite sides of the continent. Fuchs' team made slow progress and were soon well behind schedule. Meanwhile Hillary had quickly climbed the Skelton Glacier to reach the polar plateau.

Hillary established his last supply camp 800 kilometres from the Pole then made a dash for the South Pole, arriving on 4 January 1958. With summer almost over, Hillary advised Fuchs to fly out when he reached the Pole and complete his journey the following year. But Fuchs resolved to continue, and reached the Pole on 19 January. The last leg of his journey went more smoothly and he reached the Ross Sea on 2 March having travelled 2460 kilometres in 99 days.

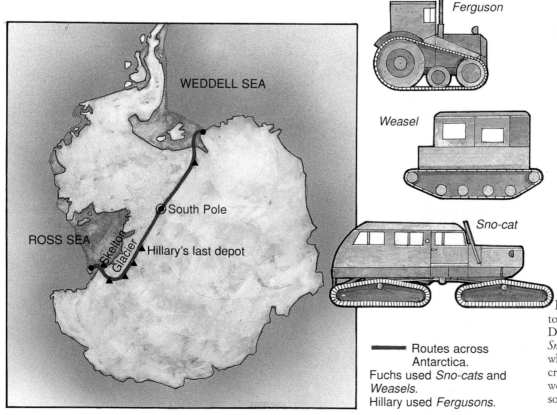

WEDDELL SEA

South Pole

ROSS SEA

Skelton Glacier

Hillary's last depot

Ferguson

Weasel

Sno-cat

—— Routes across Antarctica.
Fuchs used *Sno-cats* and *Weasels*.
Hillary used *Fergusons*.

DOG TEAMS were sent ahead to search for hidden crevasses. Despite their caution, Fuchs' *Sno-cat* fell into a deep crevasse when the snow bridge he was crossing collapsed. Metal ramps were placed under the vehicle so it could be reversed to safety.

VIVIAN FUCHS (1908-) led the expedition to cross Antarctica in 1957-8. His team was supported by Edmund Hillary (1919-), the New Zealand mountaineer who, with Sherpa Tenzing Norgay, had been first to climb the world's highest mountain, Mount Everest, in 1953.

FUCHS' TEAM drove in convoy across the polar plateau on the journey to the Pole. They made regular soundings of the ice during the trip, to find out the thickness of the ice-sheet. They established that the South Pole is situated in a gigantic ice-filled basin bordered by mountain ranges. The average depth of the Antarctic icecap is 2.4 kilometres. It contains as much water as the Atlantic Ocean.

Hillary

Fuchs

Fuchs' team drives across the polar plateau.

IN 1959 the Antarctic Treaty was signed by 12 nations. It stopped all nations' claims to territory, and declared that Antarctica should be used for peaceful research only. Today teams from many nations continue to explore Antarctica, studying weather and wildlife, and mapping the land buried beneath the ice.

TIME CHART

AD 986 Erik the Red and 15 Viking ships sail to Greenland and establish two colonies there.

1497 John Cabot discovers Newfoundland.

1553-4 Willoughby and Chancellor search for the Northeast Passage. Chancellor visits the court of the Russian Tsar in Moscow.

1576-8 Martin Frobisher searches for the Northwest Passage to China and visits Frobisher Bay on Baffin Island in search of gold.

1596-7 Willem Barents and his crew are forced to spend the winter on Novaya Zemlya.

1607-11 Henry Hudson discovers the Hudson River and Hudson Bay, but his crew mutiny and he is cast adrift in a small boat. The boat is never seen again.

1615-6 William Baffin explores Baffin Island and the Northwest Passage.

1724-42 Vitus Bering leads a team of explorers mapping the Arctic coast of Siberia.

1773-5 Captain Cook sails around Antarctica without sighting land.

1819-20 William Smith and Edward Bransfield discover the South Shetland Islands.

1821 Nathaniel Palmer sights the mainland of Antarctica. John Davis's men are first to land on the continent of Antarctica.

1831 James Clark Ross locates the magnetic North Pole on the Boothia Peninsula.

1840 Dumont d'Urville and Charles Wilkes make the first official sightings of Antarctica.

1841 James Clark Ross discovers the Ross Sea, Ross Island and the Ross Ice Shelf.

1845-7 Sir John Franklin sails in search of the Northwest Passage.

1878-9 Baron Nordenskjold completes the Northeast Passage.

1893-6 Fridtjof Nansen attempts to drift to the North Pole in the *Fram*.

1903-6 Roald Amundsen completes the Northwest Passage in his ship the *Gjoa*.

1906-18 Vilhjalmur Stefansson explores the Canadian Arctic and studies the Inuit way of life.

1908-9 Ernest Shackleton almost reaches the South Pole.

1909 Robert Peary is first to reach the North Pole.

1912 Roald Amundsen reaches the South Pole a month before Captain Robert Scott. Scott's party dies on their return journey.

1957-8 Vivian Fuchs crosses Antarctica via the South Pole.

1958 The American submarine *Nautilus* passes under the North Pole.

1967 Antarctica's highest mountains are climbed by an American team.

1968-9 Wally Herbert crosses the Arctic Ocean via the North Pole.

1978 Japanese explorer Naomi Uemura is first to reach the North Pole alone and on foot.

1992-3 Ranulph Fiennes crosses Antarctica on foot.

1912-3 Douglas Mawson narrowly escapes death on a sledging expedition in Antarctica.

1915-6 Ernest Shackleton's ship is sunk in the Weddell Sea. He reaches Elephant Island and South Georgia in an open boat.

1926 Richard Byrd flies over the North Pole. Roald Amundsen is first to reach both Poles.

1928 Hubert Wilkins is first to fly over Antarctica.

1929 Richard Byrd flies to the South Pole.

GLOSSARY

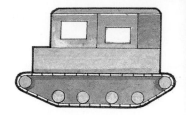

Antarctic/Arctic Circles
imaginary circles drawn around the Earth running parallel to the Equator, marking the borders of the polar regions.

Blizzard
storm with high winds blowing powdery snow.

Caribou
French-Canadian word for reindeer.

Crevasse
deep crack in glacier, sometimes concealed by snow.

Depot
camp of stores.

Equator
imaginary line around the widest part of the Earth, half-way between the North and South Poles.

Floe
floating sheet of ice.

Fiord
a long, narrow inlet of the sea with high, steep sides.

Frost-bite
condition caused by extreme cold, which destroys the tissue of the body. The ears, nose, toes and fingers are the areas of the body often first affected.

Glacier
river or large mass of ice, formed of packed-down snow. Glaciers appear to be still but in fact flow downwards very slowly.

Iceberg
large piece of land ice floating in the sea, once part of a glacier or ice shelf. Icebergs are a hazard to ships in polar waters. Only about one-eighth of an iceberg shows above the surface of the water.

Ice breaker
strong ship built to smash its way through thick sea ice.

Ice cap
mass of ice permanently covering the land in Polar regions.

Ice shelf
vast slab of floating ice attached to land. The Ross Ice Shelf in Antarctica is bigger than France.

Igloo
Inuit house or shelter, often made of ice blocks. The Inuit traditionally heated their homes with lamps which burn seal blubber (fat), or oil.

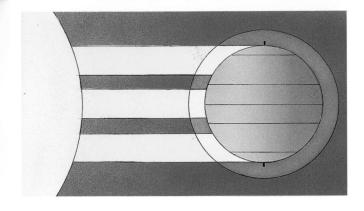

Inuit
the peoples living in the Arctic, from Alaska to Greenland. In the past Inuit were called "Eskimos". The Inuit themselves dislike this name as it means "eaters of raw meat".

Kayak
one-person canoe, made of sealskin stretched over a wooden framework.

Lapps
a hardy people living in the Arctic in Europe's far north. Traditionally Lapps (or Saami) lead a nomadic life, herding reindeer.

Lead
area of open water in pack ice.

Magnetic Poles
regions located in the Arctic and Antarctic, towards which compass needles point. These areas do not stay in exactly the same spot, however, but are constantly moving.

Northeast Passage
sea route leading from Europe to Asia via the Arctic Ocean north of Siberia.

Northwest Passage
sea route leading to Asia via the Arctic Ocean north of America.

Pack ice
blocks of sea ice wedged together to form a great mass of ice.

Plateau
area of high, flat ground.

Pole
imaginary point marking the most northerly and most southerly limits of the Earth.

Scurvy
a disease common among early sailors and polar explorers. We now know it is caused by a lack of vitamin C, found in fresh fruit and vegetables.

Sealer
seal-hunter or seal-hunting ship.

Strait
a narrow sea channel linking two large areas of water.

Whaler
whale-hunter or whaling ship.

47

INDEX